ANIMAL GIANTS

D0275987

ANIMAL GIANTS

Barbara Taylor

Foreword by
Robert Napier

KINGFISHER

Editor: Vicky Weber
Designers: Mark Bristow, Carol Ann Davis
Cover designer: Mike Buckley
Picture researcher: Rachael Swann
DTP manager: Nicky Studdart
Senior production controller: Deborah Otter
Proofreader and Indexer: Sheila Clewley
Consultant: David Burnie
Artwork archivists: Wendy Allison, Jenny Lord

KINGFISHER

Kingfisher Publications Plc
New Penderel House
283–288 High Holborn
London WC1V 7HZ
www.kingfisherpub.com

First published by Kingfisher Publications Plc 2004

10 9 8 7 6 5 4 3 2 1

WBX/0704/EUR/MA(MA)/130R400/C

ISBN 0 7534 1055 9

Copyright © Kingfisher Publications Plc 2004

A CIP catalogue record for this book is available from the British Library.
Printed in Italy

GO FURTHER...

INFORMATION PANEL KEY:

websites and further reading

career paths

places to visit

SCALE BOX

Where possible, we have tried to illustrate the size of the animals in this book by showing them next to another object, such as a human or a tree. This has not been achievable in every instance, so on some pages, there is a small scale box (see right), which gives the sizes of all animals on the page in relation to a 1.75m-tall human.

giant tortoise   Galapagos hawk

WARNING

Most of the animal giants in this book are extremely dangerous wild predators and should not be approached on any account either in the wild or in a zoo.

NOTE TO READERS

The website addresses listed in this book are correct at the time of publishing. However, due to the ever-changing nature of the internet, website addresses and content can change. Websites can contain links that are unsuitable for children. The publisher cannot be held responsible for changes in website addresses or content, or for information obtained through third-party websites. We strongly advise that internet searches should be supervised by an adult.

ABOUT THIS BOOK

As you read this book, remember that there is still a lot we do not know about giant animals and why they grow to such vast sizes. Many of the explanations for their record-breaking statistics are theories — ideas that people, especially scientists, have suggested but not proved. More scientific research and exciting new discoveries of both fossilised animals and living creatures (which are being made all the time) may change or add to these explanations in the future.

Contents

Foreword

The book you are holding is packed with fascinating pictures and information about all kinds of animal giants – truly incredible creatures that share the earth with us humans. But a word of caution! Just because these mammals, reptiles, insects and birds are giants, often big enough and sometimes mean and ugly enough to defend themselves, it does not always mean that their existence is guaranteed. It is a fact of evolution that animal giants disappear – you only need to think of the dinosaurs that lived 65 million years ago, or the woolly mammoth, a relative of the elephant, that roamed the earth 11,000 years ago. But spin forward from those faraway times and think of today. Many species you know well – the white rhino and the humpback whale, for example – are threatened with extinction. If we are not careful, they will vanish, just as the dinosaurs and the mammoths did. But the reasons will be different. The dinosaurs disappeared because of natural events, whereas many modern species are threatened because humans are either killing them, or destroying the habitats they rely on for their existence.

People often ask me whether extinction really matters. It certainly does! When a species dies out, its disappearance has a knock-on effect on other animals and plants that rely on it for their own survival. Prey animals, for example, support the balance of life in their habitat. And as the plant-eating elephant travels through the forests or across the savannah, it consumes a variety of seeds that have to pass through its digestive system in order to germinate and begin a new round of life.

There are also the artistic and the emotional reasons why extinction matters. Would you like to live in a world without giant pandas or blue whales or mountain gorillas? I most certainly would not – and I hope you would not either. That is one of the reasons why WWF, the global environment organization, is busy in more than 90 countries around the world. We work to conserve endangered species, protect threatened spaces and address global threats to the planet for the benefit of people as well as nature. As you turn the pages of *Animal Giants*, you will discover animals that are astonishing, beautiful, weird, unusual and maybe even downright horrible! But whatever you think of them, I hope you will consider what you can do to help protect them for the future of their species and our planet. After all, they have as much of a right to life on earth as we do, and we would all be so much poorer without them.

Robert Napier is the Chief Executive, WWF-UK, www.wwf.org.uk.
WWF is best known for its programmes to protect endangered species. It also strives to protect threatened habitats, and to reduce worldwide dangers to people and nature, such as climate change, forest destruction and the use of toxic chemicals.

CHAPTER 1

Largest on land

Any person standing next to one of the huge dinosaurs would barely be able to touch its knees, and its long neck would tower way up in the sky. No land animals today reach such a colossal size – and, indeed, a lot of the biggest animals have been hunted and killed by humans. Nevertheless, you may be surprised to learn that there are still elephants, bears and ostriches that look down on people from great heights, as well as snakes as long as a bus and insects bigger than mice. Sound unbelievable? Sound scary? Read on and meet some of these extreme animals. Prepare to be amazed!

Giants of ancient lands

The biggest and heaviest land animals of all time were the long-necked dinosaurs. The largest were longer than a tennis court and nearly three times taller than a giraffe. Their gigantic weight must have made the ground shake as they plodded along. One of the most colossal, *Brachiosaurus*, weighed as much as 15 African elephants! Why did they grow so big? No one can be sure, but scientists have a lot of different ideas.

▲ These three long-necked dinosaurs, *Supersaurus* (left), *Ultrasauros* (centre) and *Seismosaurus* (right), may have been the biggest of their kind. No complete skeletons have yet been found, and their exact size and weight are a matter of great debate. The *Ultrasauros* bones discovered so far may even have come partly from a *Brachiosaurus* and partly from a *Supersaurus*.

Too big to attack

You may be surprised to know that the average dinosaur was as big as an elephant and that some dinosaurs were only the size of chickens! It was the huge bulk of the long-necked plant-eaters that gave the dinosaurs their reputation for immensity. Being big definitely had its benefits, for it made it easier for the huge herbivores, such as *Brachiosaurus* and *Diplodocus*, to survive attacks by the smaller meat-eating dinosaurs. The giant survivors passed on their characteristics for large size to their offspring, which helped them survive. Proportions increased, generation after generation, until the size of the long-necked herbivores was eventually limited by the problems of finding enough food to eat and supporting the weight of a huge body.

Big eaters

The long-necked dinosaurs had plenty of plant food to eat since they could reach leaves high in the trees, and their long digestive systems could process and digest large quantities of plants, even tough ones. Inside their huge stomachs, microscopic bacteria helped the dinosaurs to break down their food, generating heat as they did so. A lot of heat in a big stomach would have speeded up the digestion, turning food into growth more quickly.

Slow movers

As they strolled around looking for food, the long-necked dinosaurs moved at about the same speed as a person walking quickly. They were far too heavy to run and would probably have broken a lot of bones if they had tried. They walked on four massive, pillar-like legs, which supported their bulk. And bulky they were, for some of them weighed over 80 tonnes. Their arched backbone braced the body rather like a suspension bridge. However, many of the bones in the skeleton were lightweight: hollow bones in the neck, backbone and tail reduced the overall weight of the body.

Small beginnings

Female dinosaurs may have been bigger than males to help them withstand the pressures of laying eggs and caring for their young. Yet even the biggest dinosaurs laid relatively small eggs – the largest ones were the size of a small melon. If they had been any greater, they would have needed thicker shells to stop them collapsing. Then it would have been difficult for the babies developing inside the eggs to get enough oxygen to keep them alive, and the babies would have found it difficult to hatch.

Ice Age giants

Dinosaurs were not the only giants of ancient lands. During the last Ice Age, which ended some 10,000 years ago, other giant mammals roamed the land. These were beasts such as hairy mammoths, which could grow up to 4.5m in height, with tusks over 5.2m long; giant ground sloths that were almost as big as a modern elephant; and giant armadillos the size of a small car. The harsh conditions may have encouraged the development of these giants, as super-size species are better at competing for scarce resources, such as food. Being large may also have helped them survive the cold, as big animals cool down more slowly than smaller ones. This is because they have a smaller body surface on the outside (compared to their huge volume inside) through which they lose heat.

◀ Long-necked dinosaurs, such as this *Brachiosaurus* (centre, right), had relatively small heads, which were large enough to collect plant food but small enough not to weigh down the long neck. They may have had a powerful heart and special muscles in the neck to pump the blood all the way up to the head, as well as valves to stop blood flowing backwards. Meat-eaters, such as *Ceratosaurus* (centre, left), had much shorter, stronger necks, with a big, powerful head to savagely bite and hold their prey.

The African elephant

All the really large land animals today are mammals, including the biggest and strongest of all – the African elephant. A large male weighs as much as 80 people! This jumbo also has the largest ears and the longest nose of any living animal. It has a large brain in relation to its body size, as we do. Elephants are highly intelligent animals with a remarkable memory.

Supporting skeleton
African elephants have an extremely strong, bony skeleton to support their colossal weight. All elephants' legs are straight and are positioned directly underneath the body, like the legs of a table. The bones in a male elephant's legs grow until it is 35 to 45 years old. In females, this growth stops at the age of about 25. As males grow through most of their lives, they may end up twice as heavy as females. Big, strong males are more likely to win fights for females.

◄ This charging elephant holds its ears out to the side in warning – to make itself look bigger and more threatening. If its ears were held flat, with the head down and the trunk folded back out of harm's way, this would show that the elephant means to finish the charge with an attack. Although elephants usually move slowly, they can suddenly speed up to 40km/h – that is much faster than a person can run!

▼ When it is born, after nearly two years inside its mother, a baby elephant weighs up to an astonishing 113kg. It is still small enough to be attacked by lions and hyenas, so it stays close to its mother and the rest of the herd. A calf drinks about 11 litres of its mother's nourishing milk every day and puts on weight very fast — at a rate of about 10 to 20kg a month. Calves continue to drink their mother's milk until they are between four and six years old.

Tusks and teeth

An elephant has only four teeth inside its mouth at any one time. Each tooth is very big, weighing more than a brick! These massive molar teeth have sharp ridges to help the elephant grind up its tough plant food. And they certainly have a job to do, for a male may eat as much as 300kg of plant material every day. The teeth come through at the back of the mouth, move slowly forwards and break up or fall out at the front. New teeth replace the old ones. At about the age of 70, an elephant's last set of teeth wears away. This means it cannot chew its food properly and its life comes to an end.

An African elephant usually has two extra front teeth, called tusks. These are made of ivory and grow outside its mouth throughout its life. The longest tusks measured 3.5m and the heaviest one weighed 117kg. Elephants with large tusks are rare today because so many have been shot for their ivory. This valuable material is easy to carve, lasts a long time and is worth a lot of money.

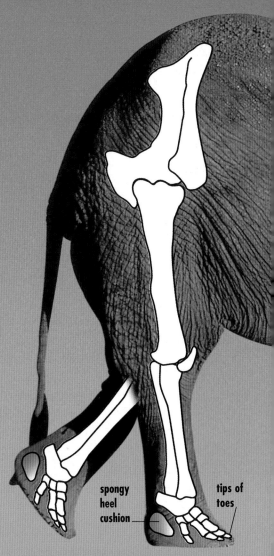

spongy heel cushion   tips of toes

▲ An elephant rests its enormous weight on the tips of its fingers and toes and a spongy heel cushion, which works like a huge shock absorber. This muffles the sound of objects underfoot, making the elephant a surprisingly silent giant.

Big ears

The size of tablecloths, African elephants' ears are three times the size of Asian elephants' ears, most likely because they live in hotter places. The elephants flap these huge ears like moveable radiators to cool themselves down. This is important, as their big bodies lose heat slowly and they cannot sweat to cool down.

African elephant

◀ Standing up to 2.8m tall on its back legs, this Kodiak brown bear, called Bart, dwarfs its keeper in a friendly wrestling match. You can see Bart's immense front claws, which are able to grow as long as a human hand. In the wild, these claws make deadly weapons but are also very useful for digging up food and making dens for the winter.

Bear facts

Imagine standing in front of a bear that weighs eight times more than you do and can stretch to a height of nearly 3m. You are unlikely ever to witness such a sight first-hand, as the largest bears – the polar bear and the Kodiak brown bear – usually prefer to avoid people in the wild. This is lucky because they have fiery tempers and can run faster than Olympic sprinters!

Ferocious force

The greatest bear ever to have walked on earth was also the largest known carnivorous mammal on land. At twice the size of the Kodiak bear, the short-faced bear was truly awesome. It lived millions of years ago in North America and probably hunted ancient camels, bison and horses. Modern wild bears are smaller than this huge beast, but they are no less fearsome. Polar bears, Kodiak brown bears and grizzly bears (a type of brown bear) are the largest meat-eaters on land today. Their size and strong bodies make them absolutely formidable predators.

Body-building diet

Polar bears are the only bears that live solely on meat; other wild bears will eat almost anything, from roots and leaves to insects and deer. Grizzly bears eat very little meat, but when they do hunt, they are terrifying. They chase large animals, such as caribou, using their strong shoulders and paws to knock the prey off its feet. They can crush the skull of their victim with a single blow, and crack open the leg bones with their powerful jaws in order to reach the juicy marrow inside.

Among the brown bears, the champion heavyweights are the Kodiak bears of Kodiak Island, Alaska, USA. They can weigh as much as a small car. Kodiak bears grow to enormous sizes because they live in a mild, moist climate with abundant food supplies. As well as having plenty of berries and plants to eat, the Kodiak bears also feast on salmon, which is rich in fat and body-building protein.

Unique giant

Despite being called 'giant', the extraordinary and unique giant panda is the second smallest bear. It is 1.6m tall – about the size of an average adult woman – and weighs up to 125kg. Many people think that the giant panda is a member of the raccoon family, but genetic tests show that it is closely related to bears, although it does not really behave like one. The giant panda does not hibernate and is vegetarian, relying on bamboo for up to 99 per cent of its food.

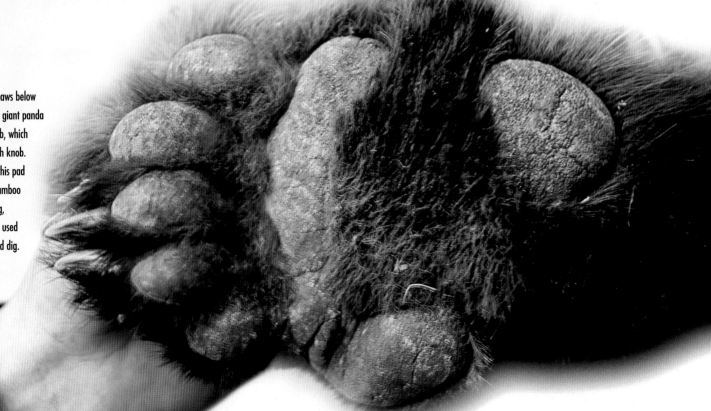

▶ On its front paws below the first finger, a giant panda has a false thumb, which looks like a tough knob. The panda uses this pad to help it hold bamboo stems. The strong, curved claws are used to climb trees and dig.

▼ A giraffe looks down on the world from the huge height of up to 6m above the ground – higher than a double-decker bus. The giraffe needs a large heart to pump blood all the way up its neck, which can grow as long as 2.4m. This graceful giant not only has a long neck, it also has a very long tongue, which can reach round to lick its eyes and ears. It uses this flexible tongue to help it strip leaves from branches high above the ground.

Remarkable body parts

From enormous horns, tusks and antlers to huge eyes, ears and noses, some animals have truly remarkable body parts. Often, the whole animal is gigantic, but small animals sometimes have extra-large features, such as bushbabies, whose massive eyes dominate their tiny faces and help them to see in the dark. Big body parts can help with all sorts of things, such as finding food, winning a mate, avoiding attack or keeping warm or cool.

Finding food

Extremely long body parts make it easier to find food in places that other animals have no hope of reaching. A giraffe's tall neck and an elephant's long, stretchy trunk allow them to get to food high in the trees. The long, sticky tongues of anteaters and woodpeckers enable them to access the narrow places where insects hide, and lap up as many tiny creatures as possible in a short time. The toucan's long bill helps it to reach fruit hanging from thin twigs too small to land on, while pelicans have large, pouch-like bills to help them catch their fishy food. The Australian pelican has the longest bill of any bird. This amazing feature grows to lengths of 34 to 47cm and can carry more food than can be held in the pelican's stomach.

▼ Giant anteaters usually extend their 60cm-long tongues into ant and termite nests. The insects stick to the tongue and are drawn back into the anteater's mouth. These unusual creatures can flick their tongues in and out about 150 times a minute and eat an incredible 30,000 insects a day.

Mega headgear

There are three types of huge headgear – horns, tusks and antlers. All of them are used for defensive purposes and for fighting rivals, while tusks may also be used to gather food. However, each one is made from a different substance and they grow in a variety of ways. Horns are made from keratin (the same material as human hair and nails); antlers are made from bone; and tusks are extra-long teeth made of a hard material called dentine. Horns and tusks usually last throughout an animal's life, whereas antlers are shed and regrown each year.

The largest horns, tusks and antlers grow on the most enormous animals. The longest horns belong to the wild water buffalo – they have a spread as wide as two grown men lying end to end. The horns are hollow, so they are not as heavy as you might think. The world's largest deer, the moose, has the biggest antlers, with a span of up to 2m. And the African elephant – the most immense land animal – has the largest tusks. The longest ones ever recorded measured an amazing 3.5m – that is about half the width of the goal on a football pitch.

▼ The gigantic front horn of a white rhinoceros can grow twice as long as a person's arm. Many rhinos have been killed for this valuable headgear and some species are in danger of extinction. The horns are used to make medicines and dagger handles.

Keeping warm or cool

Large body parts may help mammals to control their body temperature. The large ears of elephants, fennec foxes and jackrabbits act like personal radiators, giving off body heat and cooling the animal down. The musk ox grows the longest hair of any mammal. The hairs on its outer coat can reach nearly 1m long and keep it warm in its Arctic habitat.

▶ Opening its jaws for a dental check-up, this hippo shows what 'open wide' can really mean! A hippo's lips are nearly 70cm in width and the tusks in its lower jaw grow up to 50cm long. These tusks are strong enough to make holes in the side of a wooden boat, but are only used for defence or fighting rivals.

Island giants

Real, live dragons; tortoises as heavy as three people; crabs the size of cats… island giants are the fabric of legends – and nightmares. No one is sure why some island animals grow so big. It may be because there is less competition for food on an island or because there are fewer predators. Also, larger species could be better equipped to survive the sea journey from the mainland.

▲ As you can see, this giant tortoise from Fregate Island in the Seychelles is almost as tall as a small child. These tortoises were probably giants when they first reached the Seychelles, perhaps by drifting on rafts of vegetation from the African island of Madagascar. Being large, with extra fat reserves, may help them to survive dry summer seasons, when there is often little food or water.

Long lives, large size

Certain reptiles, such as giant tortoises and the world's largest lizard, the Komodo dragon, never stop growing. On islands where there is a lot to eat and few predators, reptiles can live for many years, giving them time to grow to enormous sizes. The giant tortoises of the Galapagos Islands in the Pacific Ocean may live for over 150 years, growing to more than 130cm long.

My shell is my castle

Having the space to grow is important for the world's largest land crustacean – the coconut, or robber, crab. This giant is related to hermit crabs, which live inside empty shells to protect their soft abdomen (rear end), but are then only able to grow as big as their home.

Young coconut crabs also live inside empty shells for a few weeks, but the adults abandon these borrowed shelters, which means they can become much bigger. After they have left the shell, they grow a hard case over their abdomen. When they outgrow this body casing, they moult and develop another, larger one.

Coconut trees grow well on islands, so the crabs have plenty of their favourite delicacy to eat, allowing them to reach 1m from head to tail.

Island feasts

Giant tortoises and coconut crabs are enormous, but they eat plants, not people. The Komodo dragon is not as harmless. Measuring up to 3m, it can kill large prey such as water buffalo and even the occasional unlucky human. There are no other big meat-eaters on the islands where the dragon lives, probably because large mammals could not survive the long sea journey without food. This means the dragon is the only big predator and may have grown larger by eating the pygmy elephants that lived on the island until recently.

▲ Standing so close to a Komodo dragon to get a good holiday snap is a high-risk strategy. They are not fast animals and usually rely on surprise attacks to catch their prey. However, their sharp claws are lethal and a mouth full of infectious bacteria means that even a small bite from a Komodo dragon can prove fatal.

◄ Two coconut crabs tackle a coconut with their powerful claws. Coconuts are the favourite food of these huge crustaceans and they will go to great lengths to get hold of one, even climbing trees to shake them to the ground. Coconut crabs get their alternative name of 'robber' crabs because they steal anything they can lay their pincers on.

Mighty serpents

Horrifying stories of giant man-eating snakes are common, but do such super serpents really exist? The short answer is that there are very few records of snakes measuring much more than 9m, and even then researchers disagree about the exact lengths. Some sizeable snakes, such as pythons and anacondas, are dangerous to people because of their enormity, but they do not usually attack humans. Really big snakes are not so common today because of habitat destruction and hunting.

The big six

The six biggest snakes are all boas and pythons. They are constricting snakes, which wrap their coils around their prey and kill them by suffocation. Two of these giants, the anaconda and the boa constrictor, come from South America. The Indian python and the reticulated python (or retic) come from Asia. The last two are the African rock python, and the Amethystine, or scrub, python, which comes from Australia and New Guinea. Of the 'big six', the longest is the retic, which can grow as long as a bus!

The heaviest snake is the anaconda, weighing up to 227kg – that is likely to be about five times heavier than you. Anacondas can grow to such massive sizes partly because they live in the rivers of the Amazonian rainforest, where the water helps to support their weight. They also keep growing (although at a slower rate) even when they are adults. This means that the real monsters are those that manage to escape being killed, live for a long time and grow to shocking sizes.

▶ The African rock python is the largest snake in Africa. This one is eating an antelope, which will provide the snake with enough energy to survive for several months. To help it swallow such a big meal, the snake unhinges its flexible jaws and allows its scaly body to stretch. Unlike you, the python is able to breathe whilst swallowing, because it pushes the windpipe to the front of its mouth.

▲ This enormous reticulated python needs five people to carry it. The retic is the longest snake in the world: it is widely accepted that it can reach a length of 9m, and many people claim to have seen larger sizes. The reticulated pattern of criss-cross lines on the skin of the snake camouflage it well when it is hunting. Large retics may ambush animals as big as deer and pigs, and there are even occasional reports of humans on the menu…

Big appetites

It goes without saying that big snakes need to eat a lot. Finding food is not easy for an animal that has no legs and has to lie in wait for prey to come blundering past. This is why large snakes live in places with plenty of food, such as rainforests. Here they can catch large prey, which sustains them for a long time. The anaconda, for example, can catch animals as big as caimans (see page 59), deer and even jaguars in surprise attacks. Large snakes also live in places, such as swampy waterways, where they do not have to compete with big mammals for food.

Clever hunter

Pythons have an extra trick to help them find their prey. They have heat-sensitive pits, or holes, along their jaws, which allow them to sense the hot body of a nearby animal. This helps them to find prey in the dark or among dense vegetation. Big pythons can catch prey as large as pigs, antelopes or even leopards. When any snake eats an enormous meal, its digestive system grows and becomes more efficient to help with the breakdown of food and to allow the snake to absorb as much goodness as possible.

Keeping warm

A snake is cold-blooded. This means its temperature varies with that of its surroundings and it cannot keep its body warm all the time as humans do. A large snake takes longer to heat up than a small one, which is another reason why big snakes are found in balmy parts of the world. Their bodies need to be warm for them to be active and it would take them too long to heat up in a cold place. Spending time in water also helps some giant snakes to maintain their body temperature, because the temperature of water is more constant than that of air.

▲ The prize for the longest beetle goes to *Titanus giganteus*, which grows up to 16cm long. It comes from the Amazon region of South America. Once the adult has emerged from its pupa, it lives for about three to four weeks, but does not feed. The beetle defends itself with jaws strong enough to bite through a pencil. The male Hercules beetle is longer, measuring up to 19cm, but half of its length is taken up by a long horn used for wrestling.

actual size

half actual size

Outsize insects

Insects are the most successful animals on earth, yet most of them are less than 25mm long. Their small size means they do not need much food and can fit into tiny homes. Even the biggest insects are shorter than the width of these two pages.

◄ Shown here at about half its actual size, the African Goliath beetle is probably as big as your hand. It is thought to be the heaviest and bulkiest of all insects, but it is still a good flyer. Males are usually heavier than females and weigh nearly as much as an apple.

Take a big breath

One reason that insects do not grow to huge sizes is that their breathing system would not work if their bodies were larger. Oxygen from the air enters the insects through holes along the sides of the body. The oxygen then passes through a system of branching tubes, called tracheae, and slowly seeps into the insect's body tissues. The bigger the insect, the further the oxygen has to travel inside the body. So, large insects usually have thin frames to make it easier for oxygen to reach all parts of the body. The more enormous insects are found in the tropics where oxygen spreads into the body tissue more quickly. This is because higher temperatures allow oxygen to be absorbed easily.

The body pump

To make their breathing system more efficient, insects would need more oxygen from the air and have some kind of pumping system to push oxygen around the body. Some big insects, such as grasshoppers and wetas, help to push the air around the body by squeezing their abdomens, so air is forced along the breathing tubes.

Prehistoric giants

Millions of years ago, some insects were much bigger than they are today. The largest prehistoric insect was a dragonfly, called *Meaneura monyi*, which lived some 300 million years ago and had a wingspan of up to 75cm – its wings were as wide as those of a gull. The largest modern relative of the dragonfly is the helicopter damselfly, with a wingspan of 19cm. One theory about how giant insects survived long ago is that there was more oxygen in the air at the time. Millions of years ago, the air was made up of about 33 per cent oxygen, compared with only 20 per cent today. This would have made it easier for giant insects to obtain enough oxygen to survive.

Growing bigger

Insects do not have an internal skeleton to support their bodies, as we do. Instead, they have a hard, heavy external skeleton, which is called an exoskeleton. This structure limits the size of insects, for they would not be strong enough to carry an exoskeleton big enough to cover a larger body. Also, it cannot stretch, so the young shed the covering in order to reach adult size. This process, called moulting, happens several times during the immature stage of the insect's life cycle, when it is a grub, a caterpillar, a maggot or a nymph. While moulting happens, there is nothing to support the body, so a really large insect could collapse under its own weight. Once they are adults, insects do not need to grow any more and so stop moulting.

◄ The longest insect of all is the giant stick insect from the rainforests of Indonesia. All the largest insects live in the tropics, where the warmth and food allow them to grow to large sizes. The one stretching across these two pages is lifesize. Its twig-like body makes it very hard to see when it sits on a woody plant and 'freezes' in one position.

► As long as a carrot and as heavy as three mice, this giant weta from New Zealand is a colossal kind of cricket. Wetas do not have wings and are probably too heavy to fly. The number of giant wetas has been greatly reduced by habitat destruction and predators that have been introduced, especially rats.

Colossal creepy crawlies

These giants look as though they could have come straight out of a horror movie – you definitely would not want to find one crawling over your bed! You might think of these mini giants as insects, but do not forget that there are plenty of creepy crawlies that are not insects. These range from giant centipedes and spiders to enormous worms and snails bigger than this page.

Wingless wonders

Most insects have wings, and if their bodies were too big and heavy, they would not be able to fly. Creepy crawlies that are not insects, such as spiders, do not have to bother about being light enough to fly. They run, scuttle or slide along the ground or burrow beneath the soil, which means that some of them can grow to astounding sizes.

▲ Giant centipedes can give people a very painful bite because they inject a large amount of poisonous venom. However, their poison is not normally dangerous to healthy adult humans. Fortunately, giant centipedes like this one do not tend to bite people unless they are provoked. Because their bodies dry out easily, they usually come out at night, when the air is cool and damp.

▶ Goliath tarantulas can grow as big as dinner plates, but their poison is not deadly to humans and most are shy creatures. They can, however, flick their prickly hairs at an attacker. If these barbed hairs stick in the skin, they can cause exteme irritation.

Vast and venomous – a deadly combination

The largest creepy crawlies live in warm places where there is plenty to eat. Bigger creepy crawlies can obviously catch bigger prey, but they must also be efficient predators. Giant centipedes use their poisonous claws to paralyse prey as bulky as small birds. The biggest spider is the Goliath tarantula, also called the Goliath bird-eating spider. It has the strength to pounce on prey of its own size, injecting venom from hollow fangs. Its poison is not as strong as that of some smaller spiders, but its size and strength make it a force to be reckoned with.

Limits to growth

Like insects, the size of many creepy crawlies, such as centipedes and spiders, is limited by their breathing system and by their exoskeleton. They have to moult their exoskeleton in order to grow. Sometimes this only happens when the animal is young (as in most spiders), but moulting and growth may continue in adults as well. This allows some creepy crawlies, such as female tarantulas, to grow very big, especially if they live a long time. Female tarantulas may live for 20 years or more, moulting occasionally to replace body parts (such as hairs) that have become damaged or worn out.

▲ The giant Gippsland earthworm from Australia is so big it looks more like a snake than a worm. When stretched out, this giant can measure up to 4m – that is probably three or four times your height! This earthworm is remarkable not just because it is a whopping worm, but also because it is a noisy worm. If you stamp on the ground above its burrow, it will become startled and slide rapidly through the tunnels of its earthy home, making a loud, distinct gurgling sound that you can hear 2m above, on the surface. The noise is caused by the worm sliding through a fluid that it produces to make the burrow walls slippery.

The biggest birds

The world's biggest birds are the ostrich of Africa, the emu and cassowary of Australasia, and the rhea of South America. These huge birds are all too heavy to fly, but they make up for it by being fantastic runners. The largest prehistoric birds were also flightless. They included the elephant bird of Madagascar – a slow-moving giant that weighed as much as a cow – and the giant moa of New Zealand, the tallest bird ever, which was as tall as two men.

▲ The emu can grow to a height of more than 2m, making it Australia's tallest bird and the second largest bird in the world, after the ostrich. Emus spend most of their time feeding on fruit, grasses, flowers, seeds and insects. In the autumn, the males eat as much as they can in order to build up fat reserves to last them through the breeding season. Male emus do not eat at this time as they sit permanently on their nest, incubating the eggs.

Raft birds

Ostriches, emus, rheas, cassowaries and kiwis belong to a group of birds called the ratites. The name comes from the Latin word *ratis* meaning 'raft' and refers to the flat shape of their breastbone. Other features that ratites have in common include their small wings and fluffy feathers with no barbs, or hooks, to link the sides of each feather together and make them streamlined for flight.

What big eyes

The biggest bird alive today is the ostrich. This giant stands some 2.5m tall – as high as a football goalpost – and has the biggest eye (see page 7) of all land animals with backbones . An ostrich's keen eyesight can spot predators and food up to 3.5km away.

Long necks

Ostriches, emus and rheas all have very lengthy necks to help them see great distances over the grasslands where they live. The neck of the male ostrich can be as long as 1.5m (this could be about your height) – it must be like having a built-in periscope. The flexible neck is also useful for reaching out for a wide range of food, such as leaves and seeds, on the ground and in bushes.

▲ The world's biggest birds also lay the most enormous eggs. The ostrich lays the largest egg of any living bird. It is equal in volume to about 24 hens' eggs and can support the weight of a person. But flightless birds laid even bigger eggs in the past. The egg of the elephant bird (above, left) had a volume equivalent to 220 hens' eggs or nine ostrich eggs!

Speed and power

Apart from the kiwi, ratites are all extremely big birds with large, muscular legs for running fast. The fastest sprinter of all, the ostrich, can run at speeds of up to 70km/h – faster than a horse. Most birds have three or four toes, but the ostrich has just two, which reduces the amount of contact with the ground. This lessens the dragging effect of friction (a force that would slow the ostrich down), making it the fastest creature on two legs. High speed is useful for escaping predators as ratites cannot fly away. If a hungry carnivore does get close, the powerful toes also make useful weapons. The kick of an ostrich can shatter a human skull, and people have been kicked to death by cassowaries protecting their young.

▲ The flightless giant moa from New Zealand could grow up to 3.7m tall. It was also a ratite, like the elephant bird, emu, ostrich, rhea, cassowary and kiwi. Moas were the only birds we know of without any wings at all. Sadly, these extraordinary birds were much too easy for people to catch. The biggest moas were probably hunted to extinction by the end of the 17th century CE; however, some smaller species may have survived well into the 19th century.

◄ Emus are champions of the marathon, covering great distances at a steady 7km/h in search of food and water. They can also sprint at speeds of up to 48km/h.

giraffe

Predators and prey

It is useful for a predator to be big so that it can easily overpower its prey. On the other hand, prey animals, such as ostriches, are less likely to be killed if they are large. Being big has advantages for both predators and prey.

Eat and grow large

Large animals need a lot of food to keep their bodies working. Since warm, tropical places are home to the greatest variety of living things, they have the most food available. This is why many outsize creatures, such as mega insects, live in tropical places. But any places with a good food supply may be home to animal giants. Kodiak bears, for example, live on a cold Alaskan island, but still grow to big sizes on a diet of berries and salmon.

A long life

When an animal lives and grows for a long time, it can reach a remarkable size. Male elephants are usually larger than female elephants because they keep growing for longer than females. Reptiles keep growing all through their lives and this has allowed some of them, such as the Komodo dragon and giant tortoises, to achieve huge proportions. Giant tortoises are one of the longest-lived of all the animals on earth. Some may live up to 200 years.

Little and large

Insects and other creepy crawlies are unlikely to be the first animals that spring to mind when you think about giants. Even the most massive ones are still relatively small, probably because their external skeleton and breathing system would not work in a bigger body. Small size can be helpful though. It means creepy crawlies can live in a range of places and eat all sorts of food, making them the most numerous and varied animals on earth. There is not enough space and food on earth for large numbers or a huge variety of giant animals to survive.

Go further...

For dinosaur information:
www.dinodata.net

Find out about elephants:
http://elephant.elehost.com

Watch slide shows and access all bear facts: www.bear.org

See some huge animals: www. extremescience.com/creatport.htm

Monsters We Met by Ted Oakes (BBC Books, 2003)

The Kingfisher Illustrated Dinosaur Encyclopedia by David Burnie (Kingfisher Publications Plc, 2001)

Why Elephants Have Big Ears by Chris Lavers (Orion Books, 2000)

Biologist
Studies living things. There are many branches of biology, such as zoology (animals) and anatomy (structure).

Ecologist
Looks at how living things are adapted to their environment and how they can be protected.

Palaeontologist
Studies the fossilized remains of creatures that lived long ago.

Park ranger/warden/zoo keeper
Looks after animals in wildlife parks, nature reserves or zoos.

Research scientist
Develops and tests theories.

Visit the dinosaurs and other giant animals at: The Natural History Museum, Cromwell Road, London, SW7 5BD, UK.
Telephone: +44 (0) 20 7942 5011
www.nhm.ac.uk

Observe animal giants at close range in a zoo or wildlife park, such as: West Midland Safari & Leisure Park, Spring Grove, Bewdley, Worcestershire, DY12 1LF, UK.
Telephone: +44 (0) 1299 402114
www.wmsp.co.uk

See the wonderful wildlife on the open plains of East Africa at: Serengeti National Park
P.O.Box 3134, Arusha, Tanzania.
www.serengeti.org

eagle owl

CHAPTER 2

Titans of the skies

The nearest people can get to flying like an animal is to soar through the sky strapped to a rigid hang-glider. Even though many of us would like to, humans cannot experience the tremendous power and manoeuvrability displayed by living creatures in flight. This is why giant flying birds, bats and insects are treated with such awe, and have inspired myths and legends through the ages. Nowadays, feathered wings are the most versatile and immense instruments of flight, so it stands to reason that birds such as eagles, albatrosses and vultures have the largest, most powerful wings in the world.

Giants of ancient skies

Dinosaurs were unable to fly, but pterosaurs, which were reptiles that may have been related to them, certainly could. In fact, they were the largest flying animals of all time. Pterosaurs lived alongside the dinosaurs for 165 million years and died out at the same time. The first pterosaurs were crow-sized, with sharp, spiky teeth and long tails. Eventually, these small pterosaurs became extinct, leaving pterodactyls, which were short-tailed pterosaurs, as the rulers of the skies. Some of the last pterodactyls became very large – one was the same size as a small aeroplane!

Lightweight giants

Pterosaurs had wings made of a double-sided sheet of skin supported by one extra-long finger and tough, flexible fibres, which helped to stiffen the wings and maintain their shape. This is very similar to the wings of a bat, which are also made of skin, but are more flexible and are supported by three or four fingers, not just one.

The skeleton of a pterosaur was lightweight, with thin-walled, hollow bones. This allowed faster, more efficient flight, because the reptiles were not weighed down by a heavy body. One of the largest pterosaurs, *Pteranodon*, had a 9m wingspan and weighed about the same as a large swan or a pelican, the heaviest flying water-birds alive today.

Gliders and flappers

The biggest pterosaurs had very long wings and were expert gliders, which saved energy. A number of them, including *Pteranodon*, may have lived like modern albatrosses, soaring over the sea in search of fish to eat. Smaller pterosaurs flew mainly by flapping their wings.

The wings were powered by large muscles, and could swing backwards and forwards and rotate, as well as beating up and down. Pterosaurs could probably control their flight well, using their manoeuvrable wings as well as their fingers, skull crests and webs of skin between their feet to help with steering and speed control. They probably flew fairly slowly, at similar speeds to today's birds and bats, which is no faster than 10 to 15km/h, although some of the giant pterosaurs may have been able to fly as fast as 50km/h. In all likelihood, they were powerful flyers, and may have migrated long distances in search of food or to avoid the seasonal changes in the weather.

▼ With a wingspan of up to 10m, *Quetzalcoatlus* was perhaps the biggest of all the pterosaurs. Named after the winged serpent god of the Aztecs, it was nearly twice the size of the largest known, modern flying bird. Unlike most pterosaurs, *Quetzalcoatlus* lived inland, not by the sea, and would have flown by soaring on rising currents of warm air, like today's vultures. It was probably a scavenger, feeding on the remains of dead dinosaurs with its toothless, dagger-like beak. Another idea is that it may have lived like a giant stork, wading through swamps to snap up frogs and other small animals.

Brains and hair

As well as wings, pterosaurs had two other features that probably helped them to become good flyers. One was their relatively large brain, which would have been needed to control the complex movements necessary for flight. The other was that they may have been warm-blooded, like bats and birds. A well-heated body would have kept their wing muscles warm enough for flight at all times. The remains of short, hair-like fibres have been found on the bodies of some pterosaur fossils. These provide evidence for their having been warm-blooded, because the 'hairs' would have helped the pterosaurs to keep a constant, warm body temperature.

The albatross

Soaring effortlessly over the windiest zones of the southern oceans, albatrosses are spectacular gliders. They can stay up in the air for hours without flapping their long, narrow wings. There are 14 species of albatross, but the three largest – the royal, wandering and Amsterdam Island albatrosses – are called the great albatrosses, and are the biggest of all seabirds. They have the greatest wingspan of any bird, measuring more than 3m from one outstretched wingtip to the other.

Long-haul flyers

Albatrosses spend over 90 per cent of their lives gliding over the open ocean, sometimes covering several thousand kilometres in a day. In a lifetime, they may fly over 16 million kilometres. They come to land only to nest, usually on remote islands. For this reason, they rely on the strength in their powerful wings to keep them aloft.

◀ Looking at David Attenborough sitting beside a wandering albatross chick, you can see just how big it really is. Fluffy down feathers help to keep the chick warm as it sits in the nest for nearly ten months, often covered in snow from winter blizzards. A fully grown chick weighs about 12kg, making it heavier than its parents, and the largest chick of any seabird.

► Albatrosses have long inner wing bones with extra feathers attached. The wandering albatross has 88 flight feathers – more than any other bird. The long wings help it to reach speeds of almost 90km/h. In the breeding season, wandering albatross parents may fly up to 150,000km to find food for their chick.

◄ In *The Rime of the Ancient Mariner* by the poet Samuel Taylor Coleridge, a mariner (sailor) shoots and kills an albatross, bringing bad luck to his ship. The crew dies, but the mariner lives on, wearing the albatross around his neck as a reminder of his terrible deed. The albatross drops off only when the mariner learns to respect living things. Even then, he is condemned to wander forever, telling his story over and over again.

Champion gliders

The shape of the albatross' body is beautifully adapted for fast gliding. As well as extra-long wings, they have a streamlined body shaped like a torpedo, and a short, square tail that acts as a rudder for changing direction. Their superb flying skills allow them to take advantage of rich patches of food, which are long distances apart in the ocean. They can also turn some of the food they catch into a high-energy oil, which they store in their stomach. They feed this oil to their chicks, enabling the babies to survive for long periods of time without food. This gives the adults time to fly a long way to collect the next meal.

Sea fishers

Albatrosses feed mainly on squid, cuttlefish, small fish and shrimp-like animals, but they also eat the dead bodies of animals such as seals and penguins. Like their close relatives – the petrels, fulmars and shearwaters – albatrosses have distinctive tube-shaped external nostrils, which they use partly for detecting the smell of food. They often feed at night, when their prey comes to the surface. The birds usually dip their head and powerful, hooked bill under the water to catch a meal, but some albatrosses, including the wandering and royal albatross, also dive under the surface in pursuit of their prey.

Threats to survival

Many albatrosses and other seabirds are killed each year by a type of sea-fishing called long-lining. Fishermen lay out lines up to 100km long, dotted with thousands of baited hooks. The lines float on the surface and the albatrosses swallow the hooks when they try to steal the bait. As the lines are pulled through the sea, the trapped birds are dragged underwater, and they drown. Several measures can be taken to save the albatrosses from this horrible death, such as using bird-scaring devices and weighting the lines so the hooks sink quickly.

▼ To make the best use of the wind, albatrosses glide down to the surface of the sea and then turn into the wind, which blows them back up into the air again. By gliding up and down like this, they can keep going for long periods of time without a single flap of their wings.

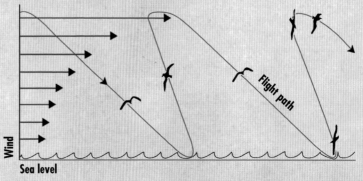

Wind

Flight path

Sea level

▶ The national bird of the USA, the majestic bald eagle, can measure up to 94cm long. It has a varied diet of live prey, such as fish, birds and small mammals. A bald eagle can kill a large salmon weighing as much as itself. Rough scales on its feet help it to keep a firm hold of the slippery fish and its broad wings give it the power to lift the heavy prey. Bald eagles also scavenge for food and will even rob other birds, such as ospreys, of their catch whenever they can.

▼ The tallest bird of prey is the secretary bird. It stands up to 1.5m tall, with a wingspan of more than 2m. Although this unusual-looking bird is a good flyer, it spends most of its time on the ground. This is why its feet are adapted for walking rather than grasping prey, and it has short, stubby toes, instead of the long talons of other birds of prey. Secretary birds eat insects, small rodents and snakes, killing the larger prey by stamping on it.

Birds of prey

The largest and most spectacular of the 400 or so species of birds of prey are the enormous eagles and the vast vultures. The biggest of all is the Andean condor, a type of vulture, which weighs about 15kg and has a wingspan of up to 3m. All vultures are scavengers, feeding on dead creatures rather than living prey. Their giant wings allow them to float high in the sky without ever needing to flap them, covering huge distances as they search for their grisly supper. Eagles are more dignified hunters. The biggest eagles, such as the harpy eagle or the bald eagle, have wingspans of up to 2m and are fierce and powerful, using their great size and strength to catch their prey.

Female heavyweights

Female birds of prey are often larger than the males, and up to twice as heavy in some species. The greatest size difference is found in birds that both chase living prey and attack creatures that are very large in relation to their own size. No one is sure why the female is bigger than the male, but it could be in order to give her more energy to lay her eggs and protect her young.

◄ The legendary roc, or rukh, was supposed to be strong enough to carry off elephants to feed to its young. The roc may have been based on either a large Madagascan eagle or the elephant bird, which lived on the island of Madagascar, off the coast of southern Africa, (see pages 24–25). Both of these giant birds are now extinct.

Clean-up crew

The huge, broad wings of a vulture allow it to glide up into the sky and drift on rising currents of hot air or strong winds. With their keen eyesight, vultures can spot prey from several kilometres away, but most find food by watching other vultures. If one bird notices a carcass, it begins to circle lower and lower. This is the signal for nearby vultures to join the feast. Some vultures eat so much at one sitting that they are too heavy to fly for a while afterwards.

Terrible talons

Eagles work harder than vultures for their meals. They too have keen eyesight, but their prey is alive and they need powerful wings to pursue, catch and carry it. They kill with their strong feet, driving huge, razor-sharp talons, like a ring of spears, into their victim. They then carry off the prey in these claws and eat it in peace.

At 4.5kg, the female harpy eagle is the strongest, heaviest eagle in the world today. She can kill prey that weighs as much as she does.

Extinct giant

The largest eagle ever was the Haast's eagle, which lived in New Zealand until about 500 years ago. Females weighed up to 13kg and had talons as big as a tiger's claws. These giants ate moas (see page 25), which were often 20 times heavier than they were. Today, most eagles attack prey that is light enough to carry, as they have to take it to a safe place to eat. There were no other large predators in New Zealand, so the Haast eagle could attack, kill and eat on the spot.

Creatures of the night sky

While we are asleep in our beds at night, a whole host of owls, bats and insects are swooping through the darkness, intent on finding a meal or a mate. The giants of this nocturnal world include owls as big as a small child and fruit bats with a wingspan as wide as your outstretched arms. Large, powerful wings enable these two kinds of night flyers to find plenty of food, and this allows them to grow to giant sizes.

Super owls

The biggest of the owls are the northern eagle owl, the great grey owl and the snowy owl. These magnificent creatures have a body size of 60 to 70cm and wingspans of over 1.5m. Female owls are often up to 25 per cent larger than males, probably so that they are better equipped to lay eggs and protect their young.

All these owls live in the extensive northern forests of America and Asia, and in the cold, bare tundra lands where their large size may help them to keep warm. In the forests and on the tundra, there are plenty of mammals and birds to eat. Despite their great size, the super owls eat a lot of small mammals, such as voles and lemmings. As the populations of these mammals go up and down, so do the numbers of the owls that eat them.

Night owls

To help them hunt in the dark, owls have exceptional hearing and eyesight. Their large eyes may account for up to five per cent of their overall body weight. The largest owls have eyes about the same size as those of a person, but they can see in the dark two or three times better than a human. Their eyes are not ball-shaped, like ours, but are huge tubes that go right back into the head and are held in place by bony structures. This means owls cannot move their eyes. To compensate for this, they have a long, flexible neck, which allows them to turn their heads almost right around in a full circle to look to the sides and behind their body.

▲ Owls, such as this great horned owl, have large eyes and huge pupils to let in as much light as possible. An owl's eyes gather perhaps 100 times more light than a pigeon's eyes, which means the owl can see over greater distances and far more clearly, especially in the dark. An owl also has an extra eyelid, which cleans and protects the surface of the eye.

▼ Northern eagle owls are very powerful predators, able to kill mammals as big as young deer. Like all owls, they have fluffy fringes on their flight feathers, which muffle the sound of their wings. Their silent flight allows them to hear their prey and then to sneak up for the attack without being heard. To grasp and kill prey, they have immensely strong legs and feet armed with needle-sharp talons. They carry small prey in their beak, but larger prey has to be carried in the talons.

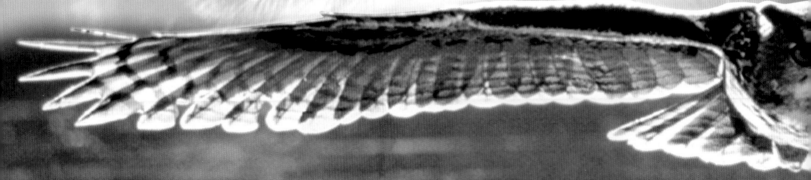

Megabats and microbats

Did you know that about a quarter of all mammals are bats? There are two main groups of bats: the 700 or so species of small, insect-eating microbats; and the roughly 170 species of much larger and slower megabats. The microbats' short wings, which they flap 11 to 18 times a second, make them terrific flyers, twisting and turning through the air as they scoop up night-flying insects. Larger wings would slow them down and make it difficult for them to catch their prey.

The megabats do not need to chase their food because they feed on fruit. To find trees with enough food growing on them, they have to fly long distances through tropical forests, so they tend to have much larger wings. Their giant wings make them slow but powerful flyers, and carry them up to 15km in one night in their search for a fruity supper.

▲ The giant Indian fruit bat is the biggest bat in the world, with a wingspan of around 1.5m and a body weight of up to 1.3kg. This megabat is also called the Indian flying fox because its furry face resembles a fox's face. During the day, the giant fruit bat roosts in trees in a huge colony, which can number up to several thousand bats. At night it flies great distances on the hunt for fruit, such as mangoes, bananas, papayas and figs.

giant Indian
fruit bat

eagle owl/
great horned owl

Butterflies and moths

Is it a bird? Is it a plane? No – it's supermoth! The Hercules moth (centre) is as big as the one on this page in real life. The biggest butterfly in the world is just as immense. It is called the Queen Alexandra's birdwing butterfly because its wings are as wide as those of a bird. Despite their huge size, these giant butterflies and moths are lightweight creatures, so they are not too heavy to fly.

Large ladies

The biggest moths and butterflies in the world are all females. This could be so that they have more energy to develop and lay their eggs. Bigger moths and butterflies are easier for predators to see; it is perhaps for this reason that the females are not at all colourful. Their camouflage makes them far less visible than males and gives them a better chance of laying their eggs in safety. The brown wings of the female Queen Alexandra's birdwing contrast sharply with the shiny blue and green wings of the male (see page 60). The males' colours may warn predators to leave them alone because they are poisonous, or could help to make them more attractive to females. The huge size and beautiful wings of the Queen Alexandra's birdwing butterflies certainly made them very attractive to butterfly collectors in the past. In fact, so many of the butterflies were collected from the wild that these stunning giants are now very rare.

Little and large

Butterflies and moths come in a huge range of sizes. The female Queen Alexandra's birdwing is about 25 times the size of the world's smallest butterfly, the dwarf blue butterfly of South Africa. This tiny cousin has a wingspan of only 1 to 2cm compared with the 28cm-wingspan of the female Queen Alexandra's birdwing butterfly. The smallest moth, *Stigmella ridiculosa*, has a wingspan of just 2mm. It looks like a dot next to the moth with the largest wingspan, the giant Agrippa moth, which measures 30cm from one wingtip to the other.

▼ This female Hercules moth has a wingspan of up to 27cm and is one of the largest moths in the world. Only the female Atlas moth, which looks very similar, is slightly bigger in overall size. All giant moths and butterflies have quite small bodies – the impression of size comes from their tremendous wingspan. The big species all live in tropical habitats, such as rainforests, where there is enough sunshine to warm up their flight muscles so that they can flap their gigantic wings. Female Hercules moths live for only a few days, relying on the energy from fat stored by the caterpillar to keep them going.

▼ Looking at this *Milionia doheityi* moth next to the Hercules moth really brings home the enormity of the giant. Both species live in the same habitat – the tropical rainforests of Papua New Guinea, a group of islands in the Pacific Ocean.

actual size

Living in harmony

One reason for this great variation in size is that big species live in different places from small species, which means they can share out the resources available in any habitat. The giant birdwing butterflies flap lazily around at the tops of rainforest trees on their powerful wings, while the caterpillars of some of the tiniest moths live right inside leaves, flowers, seeds and fruits.

Big caterpillars

Adult butterflies and moths never grow, and the female Hercules moth does not even feed. They grow only at the caterpillar stage, which means that a large adult must develop from a huge caterpillar. The young crawler spends its life eating, but its skin does not grow as fast as its body. This means that every so often the caterpillar develops a new, bigger skin and sheds, or moults, the old one. As the old skin splits, the caterpillar wriggles out, swallowing air to expand and stretch its body. When a caterpillar is fully grown, it changes into a pupa. Inside this protective case, the parts of the caterpillar's body are broken down and re-built into the adult butterfly or moth. The adult's wings are folded up inside the pupa. They do not expand until the adult emerges into the world and pumps blood into its wing veins to stiffen and flatten the wings. It may take over two hours for a big butterfly to expand its wings.

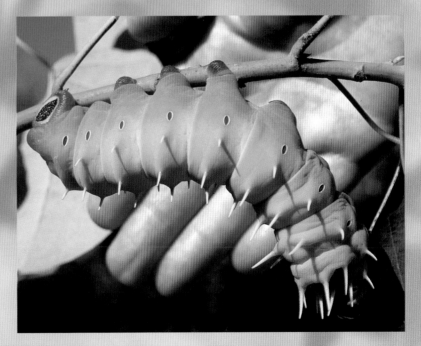

▲ The warm temperatures and good food supplies in the rainforest home of the caterpillar of the Hercules moth help it to grow up to an enormous 17cm long. Its large, fat body would make a tasty meal for any predator, but luckily it is protected by rows of sharp, yellow spikes along its back.

Indian giant fruit bat

Lightweight flyers

The bodies of flying animals cannot be too heavy or they would never get off the ground, even with very powerful wings. If you have ever let a giant butterfly or moth land on your hand, you will have felt how light they are, despite their size. Even the largest birds, such as giant owls, are not very heavy because of their thin-walled, hollow bones, some of which have air sacs inside to make them lighter.

Saving energy

Flying is tiring and uses up a lot of energy. But long or wide wings, such as those of albatrosses, vultures or giant fruit bats, allow effortless gliding. This makes it easier to fly long distances to find food or avoid bad weather.

Warm wings

Wing muscles need to be warm for an animal to fly. Birds and bats are warm-blooded, so they have warm bodies all the time. This means they can fly whenever they need to. Pterosaurs may also have had warm bodies, which would probably have helped them to develop their flying skills. On the other hand, insects such as butterflies and moths have bodies that warm up and cool down with their surroundings – they are cold-blooded. They can only fly when their wing muscles are warm enough – and the muscles needed for big wings take a lot of warming up. This is one reason why large flying insects live in warm tropical places, such as rainforests.

Massive mums

Female flyers are often even more gigantic than their male partners. The largest butterfly in the world is a female and some female birds of prey are up to twice as heavy as their mates. No one can be sure why this is, but it may help the females lay their eggs, and defend and feed their young.

Go further...

All about owls:
www.owlpages.com

Find out about albatrosses:
www.birdlife.net/action/campaigns

For answers to pterosaur questions:
www.bbc.co.uk/dinosaurs/
dig_deeper/faq_pterosaur.shtml

Fruit bat facts:
www.biology.leeds.ac.uk/staff/dawa/
bats/fruitbats/biology.html

'Birds of Prey' by Robin Kerrod
(in the encyclopedia *Nature's Predators*, Lorenz Books, 2003)

Incredible Monsters by Mike Ashley
(Robinson Children's Books, 2000)

Entomologist
Specializes in the study of insects.

Falconer
Keeps and trains birds of prey, especially hawks, and may fly them in displays for the public.

Museum worker
Classifies species (taxonomist), looks after museum collections and prepares exhibitions (curator).

Ornithologist
Studies the biology of birds.

Wildlife photographer
Photographing wildlife for books, magazines, museums, television, videos or websites.

See huge eagles, vultures and secretary birds at:
National Birds of Prey Centre, Gloucestershire, GL18 1JJ, UK.
Telephone: +44 (0) 870 990 1992
www.nbpc.co.uk

Visit the bird reserves of the Royal Society for the Protection of Birds:
The RSPB, The Lodge, Sandy, Bedfordshire, SG19 2DL, UK.
Telephone: +44 (0) 1767 680551
www.rspb.org.uk

Step into the world of tropical butterflies at:
London Butterfly House, Syon Park, Brentford, Middlesex, TW8 8JF, UK.
Telephone: +44 (0) 20 8560 7272
www.butterflies.org.uk/index.html

CHAPTER 3

Giants of the water

Giant animals that swim through the waters of oceans, rivers and lakes have a huge advantage over animals that fly through the air or plod around on land. The water pushes up their bodies, helping to support their whopping weights. Nowadays, high levels of oxygen in deep freshwater lakes and cold oceans allow animals to release more energy from their food and may enable them to grow bigger. Water is also home to a huge variety of living things, providing plenty of food for animals to grow to mammoth measurements. The biggest animal the world has ever known – the blue whale – lives in the oceans, along with other goliaths of the sea, such as monstrous squids, jumbo jellyfish and stupendous sharks. It is entirely possible that even more giants lurk in the darkness of the deep ocean. Would you like to be the one to discover them?

whale shark

Giants of ancient waters

A whole host of giant predatory reptiles swam through ancient seas and oceans. The earliest of these were large ichthyosaurs, such as *Temnodontosaurus*; then followed enormous pliosaurs, such as *Liopleurodon* and *Kronosaurus*; and finally massive mosasaurs, such as *Mosasaurus* and *Tylosaurus*. Some of these marine giants measured over 10m in length and a few may have been as long as 20m – as big as a sperm whale. The bodies of these enormous creatures were buoyed up by the water and there was plenty of food in the sea to enable them to grow to outsize proportions.

Predators of a different class

Ancient marine reptiles were far more dangerous than most of today's aquatic giants. The pliosaurs were colossal and the biggest amongst them would have been powerful enough to bite a medium-sized modern car in half! They had huge heads, perhaps measuring up to 4m long, lined with rows of sharp teeth at least as big as bananas. Large, powerful muscles drove these biting teeth into the prey.

Around 70 million years ago, mosasaurs took over from the pliosaurs as top predators and became the most dangerous creatures in the oceans. Mosasaurs were probably distant relatives of today's monster monitor lizards, such as the Komodo dragon (see page 17), and perhaps even snakes as well. Several mosasaurs reached lengths of nearly 15m, while one giant, *Hainosaurus bernardi*, was 17m long. Their unusual jaws could bend sideways to surround and crush their prey, which they then swallowed whole, eating in the same way as a modern snake.

▼ *Elasmosaurus* had the longest neck in proportion to its body of any known animal, beating even a giraffe. With at least 71 bones for support, the neck could grow up to 6m long. This allowed *Elasmosaurus* to launch a surprise attack without even moving its body, by suddenly reaching into a school of fish from several metres away.

Seeing in the dark

Ichthyosaurs (meaning fish lizards) were reptiles that looked like modern dolphins and followed a similar fish-eating lifestyle. Unlike dolphins, which are mammals, ichthyosaurs had back flippers as well as front ones, and their tail was vertical instead of horizontal. Ancient ichthyosaurs could have had eyeballs that measured more than 30cm across – as wide as bowling balls. This is even bigger than the eyes of today's giant squid, which are the largest of any living creature. Big eyes can let in and detect more light, so they would have helped ancient ichthyosaurs to hunt hundreds of metres below the surface of the ocean, where it is extremely dark.

Water babies

The biggest marine reptiles could not come on to land to lay eggs. They would have suffered like beached whales, unable to move and condemned to die from overheating, or from suffocation caused by the collapse of their lungs. There is fossil evidence of mosasaurs and ichthyosaurs giving birth to live young in the water, and it is likely that other large marine reptiles reproduced in the same way.

The blue whale

Gliding through the world's oceans is the most famous giant of all – the blue whale. Reaching lengths of over 30m and weights of 150 tonnes or more, this monumental giant is the largest animal in the world – the longest one on record measured a staggering 33.58m. Blue whales today are not as large as they were in the past because the biggest ones have been killed for their meat and blubber. Despite being a protected species, they are still endangered by pollution, hunting and being trapped in fishing nets. The sad consequence of this is that there are now probably fewer than 8,000 blue whales left.

Speedy swimmer

The combination of a smooth body, a slim, streamlined shape and 5.5m-wide tail flukes (fins) makes a blue whale a powerful swimmer. It can reach speeds of up to 50km/h, although it usually cruises at 5 to 20km/h without using too much energy. Blue whales are too fast and too big to be caught by most ocean predators, with the exception of packs of killer whales and humans.

Giant gulper

The blue whale feeds mainly on tiny, shrimp-like animals called krill (a constituent of plankton), which are less than 5cm long and drift in huge rafts near the surface of the oceans. It plunges into a mass of krill with its jaws wide open, speedily gulping a mouthful of food and water. Inside its cavernous mouth, hundreds of stiff strips of baleen hang down from the top jaw. Baleen is made from the same material as human fingernails and has fringes of hair along the edges. As the whale uses its throat muscles and tongue to force water out of its mouth, the baleen plates act as sieves, trapping vast amounts of krill on the hairy fringes. The krill is then swallowed down the whale's unexpectedly tiny throat.

▼ One of the main reasons the blue whale has been able to reach such gigantic proportions is that seawater helps to support its body. If it were stranded on land, a blue whale would die: at about 22 tonnes, the bones of its skeleton cannot support the weight of its body in the air, so the whole thing would collapse, crushing its soft internal organs. The jaws are up to 7.3m long and are the largest in the animal kingdom.

◀ A blue whale's mouth expands when it feeds because it has loose folds of skin, which look like pleats, running down from its chin almost to its tummy button. As these pleats open out, they increase the mouth size, rather like a musician opening an accordion.

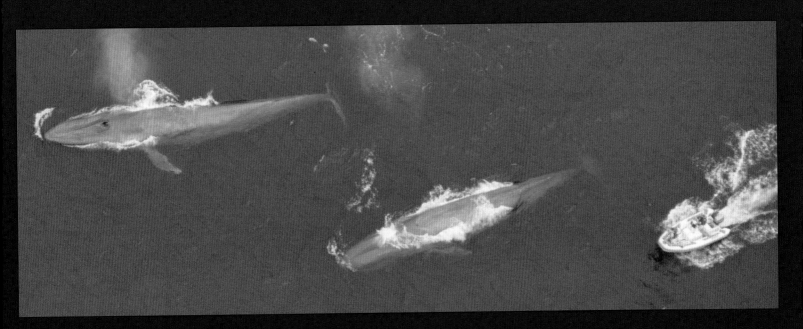

▲ We know very little about the social life of blue whales, but they are usually seen alone or in small groups of two to four individuals. This might be because they need large feeding areas to themselves. Blue whales make very loud sounds (as the loudest animals on earth, the whistles made by these creatures are louder than a jet engine), which may help whales that are far apart to keep in touch. The echoes of these loud sounds may also help blue whales to find food and navigate their way through the oceans.

World's biggest babies

At birth, baby blues weigh at least 2.5 tonnes – 700 times the weight of a human baby. They grow quickly because their mothers feed them up to 300 litres of fatty milk every day. A mother blue whale loses about one third of her body weight over the eight months that she feeds her calf. This may be one reason why females are bigger than males, because it gives them enough fat reserves to survive feeding their babies. Even though baby blue whales stop drinking their mother's milk when they are eight months old, they do not mature into adults and become able to reproduce for at least 10 years. No one knows how long they live, but scientists think they could reach 60 to 70 years or more. This is just one of the many details left to be discovered about these beautiful and gentle creatures.

Mammoth sea mammals

The blue whale might be of unrivalled size, but it is by no means the only giant of its class. In a competition for most mammoth marine mammal, there would also be a few other contenders for the top places. First behind the blue whale would be the other whales, such as humpback and sperm whales. Second would be the elephant seal and the walrus (see page 61), the largest pinnipeds. In third place would be the West Indian manatee and the dugong, which are the largest sirenians or sea cows.

▲ The largest recorded West Indian manatee was a female that reached a length of 4.1m. Manatees do not have true blubber, just a thick skin and a fat layer that provides poor insulation against cold. They live mainly in the warm tropical coastal and inland waters of the world. Manatees are very efficient herbivores, which helps them grow to big sizes. Their massive mouths are good at grasping and uprooting water plants. They also extract as much energy as they can from their food before it passes out of their body.

Fatty food

One reason that the biggest whales and seals are so large is that their bodies are surrounded by thick layers of fatty blubber, which may be more than 25cm thick. The blubber makes their bodies streamlined, stops body heat escaping when they swim in very cold polar oceans, and also acts as a food store during the breeding season, when they may not be able to feed. For about a month, whilst they are feeding their pups on rich mother's milk, female elephant seals do not eat. Male elephant seals do not eat in the breeding season either, since they are constantly defending their harem of females against rival males. They may lose up to half of their body weight in a three-month season. Migrant whales, such as grey, blue and humpback whales, also eat little during the winter breeding season, which they spend in warmer tropical waters. They use the energy they stored as body fat in the summer when they were feeding in cold polar waters.

Cruisers and chasers

Toothed whales, such as sperm whales, are usually much smaller than the baleen whales, such as the humpback whale, which filter tiny drifting plankton out of the water with fringed plates called baleen. Baleen whales do not have to do much active swimming to feed themselves. They just cruise along scooping up plankton, swallowing millions of the small animals at one meal. Toothed whales, on the other hand, must chase their prey and larger sizes could really slow them down. They catch and swallow bigger animals, such as fish, one at a time. Most toothed whales, including dolphins and white, or beluga, whales, are 3 to 6m long. But the largest of the toothed whales, the sperm whale, may reach a length of 20m.

◀ Male elephant seals are at least three times heavier than females. When threatened by male rivals or, as seen in this picture, a scientist recording a roar, the males rear up the front of their body and bellow loudly, inflating their nose and using it like a loudspeaker to make more noise.

◀ A fearless tussock bird, about as long as a person's hand, pecks for food scraps right on the nose of a female elephant seal. The females have much smaller noses than the male elephant seals and lead a much quieter life.

Lurking crocodiles

Survivors from the age of the dinosaurs, crocodiles are
superbly adapted to their environment. They lurk lazily
in the water, waiting to snap up prey in their massive jaws.
The biggest jaws of all belong to the largest reptile in
the world – the saltwater crocodile. It weighs as
much as three cars and grows over three
times longer than your bed! Almost as
immense, and just as threatening, is
the largest freshwater predator in
Africa – the Nile crocodile.

Little babies, awesome adults

When a baby crocodile hatches out of its egg, it is so small you could easily hold one in your hand. A mother crocodile holds her young in her mouth to keep them safe and to carry them from their nest to the water. She can carry up to 20 young at a time like this. The babies grow very quickly though. If they have enough to eat, they can grow roughly 30cm a year until they are about 15 years old. Then they keep growing at a much slower rate for the rest of their lives. In captivity, crocodiles grow faster than they do in the wild because they are kept in warm water and have plenty to eat.

Lazy eaters

Saltwater and Nile crocodiles are so big that they can catch large animals, such as zebras, cows, buffaloes and horses, but they mainly eat a lot of fish. They sometimes attack humans, although this usually happens only when people disturb them, especially during the mating and nesting season. Most crocodiles are timid and avoid people whenever possible. On the whole, crocodiles sit and wait for their food to come to them, as this saves energy. This sort of lazy lifestyle, along with the fact that they can store energy from their food in their tail and other parts of the body, allows a big crocodile to survive for up to two years between meals. Since they warm up and cool down with their surroundings, they do not need to use energy to keep warm, as mammals and birds do.

◄ This saltwater, or estuarine, crocodile is basking in shallow water, allowing a good view inside its gaping jaws. Crocodiles have two or three times as many teeth as a person, but these are no good for chewing food, so they swallow it whole or tear it into chunks.

Survival

Nearly 200 million years ago, crocodiles looked very similar to today's species. Apart from birds, they are the closest living relatives of dinosaurs. Crocodiles have survived for so long, and grown to such large sizes, because they are very well suited to their lifestyle. They also seem to be good at fighting disease and rarely develop cancers. Sadly, almost half of all crocodile species are endangered by loss of habitat, illegal hunting and trapping. Very large crocodiles are now rare because they are killed before they grow to their maximum size.

▼ A Nile crocodile launches an attack on an unsuspecting wildebeest drinking in the Mara river on the Serengeti plains in Tanzania. Crocodiles attack with astonishing speed, taking their victim by surprise. It is important that they overcome their prey quickly, as they cannot chase it overland.

Amazing amphibians

Frogs, toads, newts and salamanders are all amphibians, which means 'a being with a double life'. Most of them live part of their life in the water, usually when young, and the rest on land when they grow up. They can breathe through their skin as well as, or instead of, using their lungs. Some, usually young ones, have gills for breathing underwater. Amphibians tend to be small, secretive animals, but there are a few giants that break all the records!

▲ The chunky African bullfrog grows to a length of about 20cm from its snout to the end of its body. It has a very wide, gaping mouth, which allows it to catch large prey, especially other frogs.

▼ The Chinese giant salamander looks like a monster from a science-fiction film. It has a broad, flat head with no eyelids. The ridge of wrinkled skin increases the surface area for absorbing oxygen from the water of its mountain-stream habitat.

Giant salamanders

The biggest amphibians of all are two species of giant salamander, the Chinese and the Japanese giant salamanders. The Chinese giant salamander is the bigger of the two. One outstanding individual was the size of a small crocodile! Average adults measure 1.14m in length and weigh around 25 to 30kg – that is as much as a child. One reason the salamanders grow so big might be because their body processes work very slowly, saving energy and allowing them to grow steadily larger. Another reason for their size is that they live a long time – one Japanese giant survived for 55 years in captivity. Unfortunately, the salamanders are hunted for food and for use in traditional medicines so they are now rare.

▶ The body of the giant cane toad measures up to 30cm — this is about ten times bigger than the smallest toad, the oak toad. Adults have large poison glands on their shoulders and smaller ones all over the body. Their poison can kill mammals, such as dogs, and is harmful to humans, especially small children.

◀ The Goliath frog is the world's largest frog. It was once common in the rivers of tropical western Africa. Nowadays, these amphibians are threatened with extinction as a result of habitat destruction and excessive hunting.

Monster frog

Around 90 per cent of the world's amphibians are frogs and toads. In contrast to salamanders, which have long tails, frogs and toads have no tail at all. The difference between frogs and toads is rather blurred. Frogs usually have a smooth skin, long back legs, webbed feet and live by water. They move by hopping, although some can climb trees. Toads have a more warty skin than frogs and prefer to live on the ground, moving about by crawling.

Most frogs would fit into the palm of your hand, but there is a real giant with a body longer than this page. Called the Goliath frog, the largest one ever recorded measured 87.63cm, including the very long legs. It weighed as much as a large pet cat! The Goliath frog comes from warm places in western Africa, where there is plenty of food to enable it to grow to vast proportions.

The toads' new abode

The biggest toad in the world is the cane, or marine, toad. Females often weigh more than a bag of sugar and, in captivity, may reach a length of 24cm and a weight of 2.5kg. These massive toads originally came from tropical America, but were introduced into Australia to eat pests that were destroying the sugar cane crops. Unfortunately, there were few predators in Australia to eat the toads, so their numbers grew fast. In some areas, they have reached plague proportions, carpeting roads in their thousands. As well as eating the insect pests, the cane toads eat a lot of the native wildlife. Introducing animals from one country to another can have terrible consequences, especially when they are giants with huge appetites.

Mega sharks

If you think that the biggest sharks are also the most dangerous hunters, you would be wrong. The great white shark, a truly dangerous creature, is one-third of the size of the most immense shark in the world, the whale shark. Equal in mass to a double-decker bus, this fish is a genuine giant.

Gentle giants
The whale shark is not only the most gargantuan of all sharks, it is the biggest fish too. The most enormous one ever recorded was 13.5m. The second largest fish is also a shark, the basking shark, which grows up to 12m long. Even though they are big enough to swallow humans whole, these gentle giants are harmless.

A matter of size
Strangely, the most gigantic fish eat the tiniest creatures in the sea! Both the whale shark and the basking shark feed largely on plankton (tiny plants and animals that drift near the water's surface). Plankton is rich in energy because it is at the beginning of the food chain, much like grass is on the land.

The great white feeds on fish and seals, which are further up the food chain. Energy is lost at each link in the chain as it is used to fuel the life processes of the animal doing the eating. This means there is less energy left for the great white shark, so it cannot grow as large as the basking or whale shark.

Feeding habits
The plankton-eaters use very little energy to catch their food, which is another reason why they can reach such big sizes. They open their large mouths to let water in and then sieve food from the water as it flows back out over their gills. The food is trapped on a fine mesh of filters, a bit like combs, that are attached to the gills. Almost nothing but water gets through these filters. The basking shark filters over 1.5 million litres of water in one hour. That is as much water as there is in an Olympic-size swimming pool!

◄ Great white sharks attack using a high-speed dash and are powerful enough to eat a whole seal in one bite. Attacks on people may happen because the shark mistakes them for seals.

◄ This snorkeller must have had a shock when he looked beneath the surface! Whale sharks are harmless to people. The only danger is being scraped by their rough skin, which is like sandpaper, or being knocked by a sideways sweep of the huge tail.

► This plankton is the sort of food that the larger sharks eat. It is made up of microscopic plants together with minuscule, shrimp-like animals, tiny worms, fish eggs and the young of crabs and barnacles.

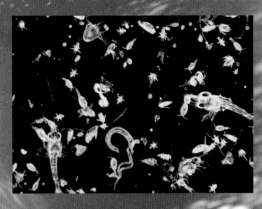

Phenomenal fish

Apart from sharks, the biggest fish range from the weighty ocean sunfish, which can top two tonnes, to the oarfish, which is able to grow as long as four cars. There is plenty of food in their aquatic environment to sustain these giants, and the water supports their immense bodies. These factors, along with their fast growth and long lifespans, mean that super sizes are easily achievable for water dwellers. Unfortunately, their size also makes them attractive to human predators, so numbers of big fish, such as tuna, have declined dramatically in recent years.

▲ The largest ray, the manta ray, usually has a wingspan of up to 7m, but the largest recorded width is about 9m. Its nickname is 'devil ray' because of the horn-like fins on its head. Like the whale shark and blue whale, mantas are gentle plankton-eating giants.

Plankton harvest

Many giant ocean fish, including the manta ray, feed on tiny plants and animals called plankton, which drift in abundance near the sea's surface. Plankton is full of energy and easy to catch, which makes it possible for large fish to develop. *Leedsichthys*, the largest fish ever to have swum the oceans, was a plankton feeder. It lived during the time of the giant dinosaurs, about 155 million years ago, and could have reached a length of between 15 and 30m. No one has yet discovered a complete skeleton of this monster fish, so it is difficult to be certain of its actual size.

Ever smaller

Beluga sturgeons of the Caspian Sea are on the verge of extinction owing to pollution of their water habitat and over-fishing for their valuable eggs, which make caviar when preserved in salt. In the past, beluga sturgeon weighing over 1,000kg were recorded, but average weights today are as low as 20kg.

Disappearing sea giants

In the last 50 years, so many fish have been caught that 50 to 90 per cent of some large species have disappeared completely. The problem is that many fish are killed when they are young, before they are able to reproduce and build up the next generation. Also, modern fishing methods are so efficient that nets and lines used to catch one kind of fish, trap and kill many other, unwanted sea creatures.

◄ This woman might make it look easy to carry a tuna fish, but do not be fooled! An average weight for a tuna is up to 45kg, and giant tuna can weigh over 180kg, with a maximum weight of about 600kg – about 15 or so times your weight. These remarkable fish grow rapidly and live perhaps as long as 30 years, which enables them to reach gigantic proportions. The only predators that dare to attack these tremendous tuna are some sharks, whales and people.

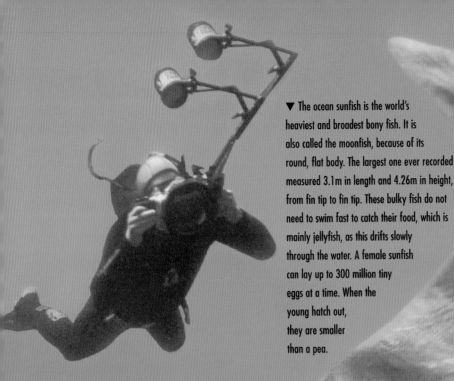

▼ The ocean sunfish is the world's heaviest and broadest bony fish. It is also called the moonfish, because of its round, flat body. The largest one ever recorded measured 3.1m in length and 4.26m in height, from fin tip to fin tip. These bulky fish do not need to swim fast to catch their food, which is mainly jellyfish, as this drifts slowly through the water. A female sunfish can lay up to 300 million tiny eggs at a time. When the young hatch out, they are smaller than a pea.

Water difference

Freshwater is less dense than salty water, so provides a little less support for the bodies of its inhabitants. It could be partly for this reason, that fish living in rivers and freshwater lakes tend to be smaller than the creatures that swim in the sea. Other reasons for the size difference could be that there is less food and space available in many freshwater habitats than in the sea. Some giants, such as sturgeon and salmon, live and feed in saltwater, but swim hundreds of kilometres up rivers to lay their eggs.

River giants

The largest fish to spend its whole life in freshwater is the Mekong giant catfish, or pla buek. This rare fish can weigh up to 300kg and grow as long as 3m. It is threatened by heavy boat traffic, extensive over-fishing and destruction of its breeding grounds in the Mekong river, which runs through southeastern Asia. Other giant catfish include the European or wels catfish, which once reached enormous lengths of over 4.5m and weights of more than 300kg. Nowadays, the largest of these fish reach lengths of only 2m and weights of 90kg.

Super-size squid

Squid range in size from tiny creatures the length of a thumbnail, through the 16m-long giant squid, to the colossal squid. If recent estimates are correct, it is feasible that the monstrous colossal squid could grow to almost twice the length of a giant squid.

Body beautiful

Squid are related to octopuses and cuttlefish. They have a long, streamlined body, a large head, well-developed eyes and a poisonous, beak-like mouth ringed by ten long arms, called tentacles. Two of the tentacles are much longer than the others and have suckers, or sometimes sharp claws, on the ends. The squid use these extra-long tentacles to grab prey. The body of most species is strengthened by a horny internal shell, called a gladius, which is shaped like a feather.

▲ Scientists gather a lot of information about the giant squid from the specimens washed up on beaches. It is hard to gain an insight into their behaviour as they have never been observed in their natural environment. Researchers are desperate to film the giant squid and send cameras into the abyss on deep-diving submersibles and sperm whales to try to catch this squid sensation.

▶ Scientists estimate that a fully-grown colossal squid could have a mantle (body) length of 4m. If the body grows in the same proportion as a giant squid, it could have tentacles reaching 25 to 30m — that is nearly the length of a tennis court!

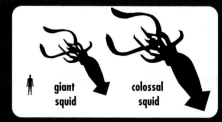

giant squid

colossal squid

Colossal squid

In 2003, fishermen in the icy Ross Sea of Antarctica became the first people ever to see a colossal squid alive. It was feeding on a fish caught on their fishing lines, which were floating on the surface. Scientists estimate that this squid, which had a mantle length of 2.5m, was about half of its full size, so it could have grown much bigger than a giant squid. The colossal squid has a huge beak and unique rotating hooks on clubs on the end of its tentacles – not something you would wish to bump into when you go for a dip in the sea.

▼ A scientist examines the eye of the juvenile colossal squid caught in April 2003. Research to date suggests that the giant squid has the largest eyes of any living creature – they can grow to the size of a dinner plate. No one knows the eye-size of a fully grown colossal squid, but it is sure to be immense.

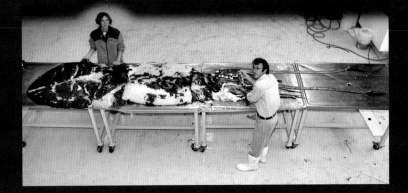

Mysterious and huge

At least ten species of large squid, over 2m long, patrol the world's oceans but as far as we know, none comes close in size to the colossal squid or the giant squid. These two mammoth creatures live deep down in the black depths of the oceans and very little is known about their mysterious lives. No one has ever seen one in its natural habitat. We can piece together information about them only from eyewitness accounts of enormous squid seen from ships, or from tentacles or bodies brought up to the surface in fishing nets or washed up on the shore. Sperm whales hunt these great squid and have sometimes been found with massive tentacles in their stomachs and sucker-shaped scars on their skin. Some scientists believe that the whales injure or even kill these super-size squid with a focused beam of sound.

◄ The Japanese spider crab is named after its long legs that look like a spider's legs. It lives in water as deep as 300m, in the Pacific Ocean off the coast of Japan. It moves slowly over the ocean floor on its spindly legs, scavenging for animal remains or feeding on live molluscs, crustaceans and worms.

Sea monsters

Real sea monsters are far more extraordinary than those you read about in stories or legends. The ones you see on these two pages are all invertebrates – animals without an internal bony skeleton – which can grow very large in the ocean with the support of the saltwater. It is unlikely that we know of every giant lurking in the myterious depths – these discoveries are still waiting to be made.

Mammoth molluscs
Several invertebrate giants, such as the giant octopus and giant clam, belong to a group of animals called molluscs, many of which have a soft body with a hard casing for support and protection. The super-size squids (see pages 54–55) and the giant octopus are both the biggest molluscs and the largest and cleverest invertebrates. Octopuses are thought to be as intelligent as a pet cat! They have no shell, so are very flexible in water, and are fast-swimming hunters with eight arms covered in suckers for swimming, gripping prey and fighting.

Super stinger

The tentacles of the world's largest jellyfish, the Arctic lion's mane jellyfish, are armed with poisonous stings instead of suckers. When prey (such as small fish, plankton or even other jellyfish) swim into its long, trailing tentacles, they are injected with a paralyzing poison, called venom. This stops them escaping while the jellyfish feasts on them.

Jellyfish were one of the first animals to live on earth and they have been swimming through the world's oceans for over 600 million years. Nowadays, there are at least 200 different kinds of jellyfish, ranging from minis the size of a fingernail to jumbo jellies, such as the lion's mane.

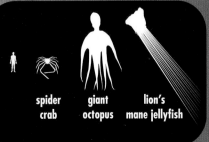

spider crab   giant octopus   lion's mane jellyfish

◀ The world's largest octopus is the shy Pacific giant octopus, which has an armspan of 2.5 to 4m (the record is 9.6m). Females have 280 suckers on each of their eight arms, making an extraordinary 2,240 suckers in total! To protect its soft body, the giant octopus lives in rocky dens, reaching out with its long arms to grab crabs, smaller octopuses and shellfish.

▲ The incredibly long, delicate tentacles of a lion's mane jellyfish trail out behind its body for up to 30m. With their tentacles fully extended, three of these massive jellyfish would stretch the length of a football pitch! At up to 2.28m wide, the body of the lion's mane is rather smaller than the tentacles, but still wider than the height of a man.

Longest legs

Crabs have also existed for a long time. Their basic body plan has stayed much the same for over 200 million years. The largest crab alive today is the Japanese spider crab, which has a legspan of over 4m – that is nearly the length of a minibus. Like all crabs, it has 10 legs, not the eight legs characteristic of spiders.

Crabs belong to a group of animals called crustaceans, whose bodies are protected and supported by a hard, crust-like cover. In order to get bigger, they have to grow a new, larger body casing and shed, or moult, their old one. Like Goliath tarantulas (see pages 22–23), crabs continue to moult as adults, which allows them to grow throughout their lives, and reach larger sizes. However, they cannot grow too big, as their body casing would become so thick and heavy that the giants would not be able to move. It would also be difficult for a very large crab to stop its body collapsing when it moulted.

SUMMARY OF CHAPTER 3: GIANTS OF THE WATER

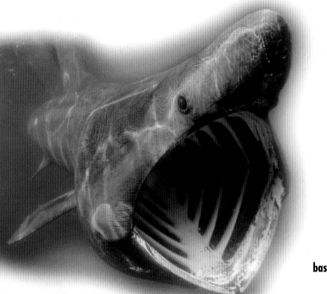

basking shark

Special support
The biggest creatures alive today, such as the blue whale, the whale shark, and the giant squid, all live in the vast spaces of the world's oceans. Here the water pushes up against their bodies from below, supporting their massive weights. (You may have noticed how the water makes your body feel lighter when you swim in a swimming pool or in the sea.) If these huge sea monsters leave the water, they cannot support the weight of their heavy bodies, which slowly collapse.

Food for giants
The mightiest water giants feed on the smallest water creatures – the plankton that drifts near the oceans' surface. Plankton is often called the 'grass of the water' because it is the start of most ocean food chains, like grass on land. There is an incredible amount of plankton floating in the sea and it is rich in energy, allowing animals, such as baleen whales, to reach immense sizes.

Big mates, long lives
Large sizes may help both male and female sea giants to survive and have larger offspring. Bigger male monsters win battles with other males for females, while enormous females have more energy reserves to feed and care for their young. With fast or continuous growth and long lifespans, the young can reach extraordinary sizes.

Go further...

For more on the ocean sunfish visit: www.oceansunfish.org

Find out about the giant squid: www.giantsquid.org

Read about whales: www.enchanted learning.com/subjects/whales

For information about sharks and rays visit: www.sharktrust.org

Monsters of the Deep
by Saviour Pirotta (Wayland, 1995)

The Blue Planet by A. Byatt, A. Fothergill, M. Holmes (BBC, 2001)

Whales by Phil Clapham (Colin Baxter Photography, 2001)

Conservationist
Works to preserve wildlife habitats, save rare species, and find ways for people and animals to live together.

Ichthyologist
A biologist who chooses to concentrate on the study of fish.

Marine biologist
Studies sea creatures and how they live in the ocean environment.

Marine mammal scientist
A variety of careers is available such as: educator, researcher, animal trainer, field biologist, film-maker.

Oceanographer
Studies the oceans.

Watch whale sharks and manta rays swimming past the biggest panoramic window in the world at: Ocean Expo Park, Ishikawa 424 Motobu-cho, Okinawa 905-0206, Japan. Telephone: +81 (0) 980 48 2741 www.ocean-park.go.jp

Experience the wonders of the underwater world at: London Aquarium, County Hall, Westminster Bridge Road, London SE1 7PB, UK. Telephone: +44 (0) 20 7967 8000 www.londonaquarium.co.uk

Explore the ocean creatures at one of the many sealife centres in Europe: www.sealifeeurope.com

Glossary

abdomen
The lower or rear part of an animal's body, which contains its digestive, reproductive and waste disposal (excretory) systems.

abyss
The vast and inky black depths of the oceans.

amphibian
A cold-blooded animal with a backbone, such as a frog or a salamander, which lives on land and in water. Amphibians depend on water for breeding and do not have a scaly skin.

antlers
The branching, bony structures growing from the top of a deer's head. Apart from reindeer, only male deer have antlers.

Arctic
The region around the North Pole, consisting of the Arctic Ocean and the tundra lands.

bacterium (plural: bacteria)
A simple, one-celled, microscopic lifeform.

baleen
A tough, horny substance, which forms fringed plates that hang from the top jaws of baleen whales, such as blue, fin and sei whales, and are used to filter food from seawater.

blubber
A thick layer of fat between the skin and muscles of sea creatures such as whales, seals and polar bears. It helps them to keep warm and acts as a food store.

breeding season
The time of year when animals find a mate and have young.

camouflage
Colours or markings that allow an animal to blend into surroundings to avoid being seen.

carnivore
An animal that eats meat.

cold-blooded
An animal whose body temperature is the same as that of its surroundings.

constricting snake
A snake that coils its body around its prey. The animal, unable to breathe, dies of suffocation.

crustacean
An animal without a backbone that lives mainly in water and has a tough, chalky body case, jointed legs and two pairs of antennae.

dentine
A hard substance that makes up the main part of the teeth of animals with backbones.

digestive system
The tubes and organs in which food is broken down so it can be absorbed into the body.

exoskeleton
A hard shell or body casing that protects and supports the body. Many invertebrates, such as insects, spiders, clams and crabs, and a few vertebrates, such as turtles and seahorses, have exoskeletons.

anaconda constricting a caiman

male Queen Alexandra's birdwing butterfly

Ice Age
Period of cold when ice covers a lot of the earth's surface. There have been several Ice Ages: the last one ended about 10,000 years ago.

ichthyosaur
An extinct reptile that looked like a dolphin and lived in the sea at the time of the dinosaurs.

insect
A small animal without a backbone that has three parts to its body and six legs. Most insects have wings and can fly.

insulation
Something that slows down the loss of heat, such as fur, feathers or blubber.

invertebrate
An animal with no backbone.

ivory
A type of dentine that makes up the tusks of animals such as elephants and walruses.

keratin
A horny material making up horns, hair, nails, fur, hooves, birds' bills and reptiles' scales.

krill
Tiny crustaceans that swim in large shoals on the surface of the sea.

life processes
The body processes common to all living creatures, such as moving, feeding, breathing, excreting, growing and reproducing.

mammal
A warm-blooded animal with fur or hair and a backbone. Mammals breathe air and feed their young on mother's milk.

manoeuvrable
Able to move quickly and with flexibility.

extinction
When a whole species of living things dies out and disappears forever.

fossils
Remains of living things, preserved in rocks.

gills
The part of the body used by some water animals to take oxygen from the water.

gladius
A stiff structure that supports a squid's body and forms a surface for muscle attachment.

habitat
The area in which an animal lives.

herbivore
An animal that eats only plants.

hibernation
A period of deep sleep, which helps certain animals to survive winter when food is scarce.

mantle
A fold of skin covering the body of molluscs.

marrow, bone
A soft, jelly-like substance, rich in nutrients, which fills many bones.

migration
The annual journey made by some animals to find good weather, food or a place to breed.

molar tooth
A wide tooth at the back of a mammal's jaw, with ridges for grinding and crushing up food.

mollusc
A soft-bodied animal without a backbone, whose body is often protected by a hard shell.

moulting
The process of shedding an outer body layer, such as fur, feathers or skin. Animals with exoskeletons have to moult in order to grow bigger as their exoskeletons do not grow as fast as their bodies.

periscope
An instrument made with mirrors and a long tube to see things otherwise out of sight.

pinniped
A group of sea mammals that includes seals, walruses and sealions.

plankton
Microscopic plants and animals that drift near the surface of oceans and lakes.

predator
An animal that hunts and kills animals for food.

prey
An animal that is hunted and eaten by other animals (predators).

protein
The chemical substances made by each cell in a living thing. They are needed as a building material or to control the chemical processes in cells.

pupa (plural: pupae)
The resting stage in the life cycle of certain insects, during which the body parts of the adult are built up inside a protective case.

rainforest
A dense, equatorial forest that is hot and wet all year round.

ratites
A group of flightless birds that has a breastbone without a keel (a narrow ridge on the breastbone of flying birds for muscle attachment) and fluffy feathers with no barbs.

reptile
A cold-blooded animal with a backbone and a scaly skin. Reptiles reproduce on land, mainly by laying eggs. The main reptile groups today are: snakes and lizards; tortoises and turtles; crocodiles and alligators.

scavenger
An animal that feeds mainly on animal remains.

sirenians
A group of sea mammals, also called sea cows, with a smooth, hairless body and paddle-like front limbs. It includes three species of manatees and one species of dugong.

skull crest
A bony structure sticking out of the top of the head. In pterosaurs, probably used for balance or display.

species
A particular type of living thing that can mate with others in the species to produce young.

streamlined
A slim shape that allows air or water to flow around the animal, enabling it to move fast.

submersible
A small submarine for working deep in the sea.

talon
The sharp, curved claws used by birds of prey to kill their victims.

tentacle
A long, flexible, arm-like structure near an animal's mouth, used for catching food and sometimes for moving as well.

trachea (plural: tracheae)
The tube through which air flows into the bodies of invertebrates. In vertebrates, the trachea, or windpipe, is the airway leading from the throat to the lungs.

tropical areas
Parts of the world near the Equator, where it is usually hot all the time.

tundra
Frozen lands around the polar regions, where it is too cold for trees to grow.

tusk
A long, pointed tooth that sticks out of the mouths of animals such as walruses and elephants.

valve
A structure that controls the flow of blood, so it moves in one direction and not backwards.

venom
A poisonous fluid in the bite or sting of animals such as snakes or jellyfish.

vertebra (plural: vertebrae)
One of the bones that link together in a flexible chain to form the backbone of vertebrate animals.

vertebrate
An animal with a backbone, or spine.

warm-blooded
Being able to keep the body at the same warm temperature all the time. Only birds and mammals are warm-blooded.

a walrus (right) and a California sealion (left) playing together

Index

Acknowledgements

The publisher would like to thank the following for permission to reproduce their material. Every care has been taken to trace copyright holders. However, if there have been unintentional omissions or failure to trace copyright holders, we apologize and will, if informed, endeavour to make corrections in any future edition.

Key: *b* = bottom, *c* = centre, *l* = left, *r* = right, *t* = top

Front cover (*left to right*) Brandon Cole/Nature Picture Library, Frank Lane Picture Agency/ © Minden Pictures, Steve Bloom; 1 Roland Seitre/Still Pictures; 2–3 National Geographic Image Collection/Michael Nichols; 4 Silvestris Fotoservice/NHPA; 7 Frank Lane Picture Agency/ © Minden Pictures; 8*tl* © John Sibbick; 8–9*c* © John Sibbick; 10*bl* M. & C. Denis-Huot/Still Pictures; 10–11*c* © Martyn Colbeck/Oxford Scientific Films; 11*tr* © Martyn Colbeck/Oxford Scientific Films; 12 Joel Sartore/National Geographic; 13 © Adrian Warren/Ardea.com; 14*bl* Whittaker/Frank Lane Picture Agency; 14*cl* and 15*bc* Mark Philips/Science Photo Library; 15*tr* © Nigel Dennis/NHPA; 15*br* Bettman/Corbis; 16*tl* © Nik Wheeler/Corbis; 16–17*c* Roland Seitre/Oxford Scientific Films; 17*tr* Jurgen Freund/Nature Picture Library; 18*tr* © Gus Christie/Wild Images/RSPCA Photolibrary; 18–19*c* © Albert Visage/Frank Lane Picture Agency; 20*tl* © Nick Gordon/ARDEA; 20*bl* Natural History Museum, London; 20–21*c* © The Natural History Museum, London; 21*br* Mark Moffet/Minden Pictures; 22*tl* © Tim Martin/Wild Images/RSPCA Photolibrary; 22–23*c* Oxford Scientific Films; 23*tr* ANT/NHPA Limited; 24*tl* Martin Harvey/NHPA; 24–25*c* Medford Taylor/National Geographic Image Collection; 25*tl* © Chris Hellier/Corbis; 25*tr* George Bernard/Science Photo Library; 26*tl* Mark Philips/Science Photo Library; 27 © Gerard Lacz/Frank Lane Picture Agency; 28–29 © John Sibbick; 30*bl* Ben Osborne/Nature Picture Library; 30*tr* Mary Evans Picture Library; 31*tr* © Wolfgang Kaehler/Corbis; 31*br* Mark Bristow; 32*bl* James Carmichael/NHPA Limited; 32–33 M. Watson/Ardea.com; 33*tc* By Edward Julius Detmold, British Library, London, UK/Bridgeman Art Library; 34–35*b* Dietmar Nill/Nature Picture Library, *c* Frank Lane Picture Agency/© Minden Pictures; 35*tr* Stephen Dalton/NHPA Limited; 36*cl* © Premaphotos; 36–37*c* Oxford Scientific Films; 37*br* Oxford Scientific Films; 38 J & A Scott/NHPA Limited; 39 Jurgen Freund/Nature Picture Library; 40–41 © John Sibbick; 42*bl* © Doc White/Seapics.com; 42–43*c* C. Neil Lucas/Nature Picture Library; 43*t* © Flip Nicklin/Minden Pictures; 44*tl* Brandon Cole/Nature Picture Library; 44–45*c* Fred Bruemmer/Still Pictures; 45*b* Brian Hawkes/NHPA Limited; 46 ANT/NHPA Limited; 47 J & A Scott/NHPA Limited; 48*tl* Clem Haagner/Ardea.com; 48*b* Ken Lucas/Ardea.com; 48–49*c* Daniel Heuclin/NHPA Limited; 49*tr* Staffan Widstrand/Nature Picture Library; 50*bl* Kev Deacon/Ardea.com; 50–51*c* Valerie Taylor/Ardea.com; 51*tr* © Douglas P. Wilson, Frank Lane Picture Agency/Corbis; 52*tl* © Flip Nicklin/Minden Pictures; 52*b* Ron Giling/Still Pictures; 53 © Richard Herrman/Seapics.com; 54*tl* Conrad Maufe/Nature Picture Library; 54–55*c* © Jurgen Ziewe; 55*c* © New Zealand Herald; 56*tl* Pat Morris/Ardea.com; 56–57*c* Jeff Rotman/Nature Picture Library; 57*tr* © Stuart Westmorland/Corbis; 58 Alan James/Nature Picture Library; 59 © Martin Wendler/NHPA Limited; 60 © Daniel Heuclin/NHPA Limited; 61 Joseph H. Bailey/National Geographic Image Collection; 64 Anup Shah/Nature Picture Library.

The publisher would like to thank John Sibbick for his excellent illustrations, David Burnie for his expert assistance, Peter Denton of the WWF for his patience and efficiency, and, of course, Purple Carol for her creativity.

The author wishes to thank Vicky Weber for her enthusiasm and support through this challenging project.